THE SWEET SPOT

Discovering Happiness Beyond
Strengths and Weaknesses

Ian Gregory

Gratis
Publishing
1178 Broadway
3rd Floor #3478
New York, NY 10001

www.gratispublishing.com

Copyright © 2023 by Ian Gregory

All rights reserved.

No portion of this book may be reproduced in any form without written permission from the publisher or author, except as permitted by U.S. copyright law.

contents

1. Sweet Spot — 1
2. Ian's Story — 6
3. Lifelong Growth — 19
4. Strengths — 24
5. Weaknesses — 30
6. Using Strengths and Weaknesses For Growth — 36
7. Wiring and the Brain — 45
8. The Need to Change — 53
9. The Plan — 57
10. Bringing the Plan to Life — 77
11. Why Not You? — 89
12. A Warrior's Life — 91

Chapter One
SWEET SPOT

I wanted to start this book by saying: I'm happy. I have a great life that I enjoy every day. I'm married to the sexiest best friend anyone could ask for. I enjoy every one of my kids and grandkids, and I have cultivated great friends that are honest and open, and we are able to have conversations that most people couldn't.

I am co-owner of my own leadership organization called Leadership In Action (LIA), and we are about training and development of current and future leaders for organizations and individuals. We have been in business for over 18 years, and I am extremely proud to say that we have been hired back, at least once, by every organization that we have served and grown.

I love helping people grow themselves. There is nothing like being in front of someone when the light goes on and they "get it." That has driven me for most of my adult life–that I can be a teacher, coach, mentor and/or friend and it can result in another person's growth. I get up every day excited because I can make a difference in someone's life, even if it is only for the couple of minutes that we have spent together.

• • • • • • • • •

This book can work for everyone. It levels the playing field, so anyone that is willing to take a good look at themselves and is willing to put in a little work can be the "winner" they have always wanted to be. It doesn't matter if life is fair or not. That being said, it has taken me a long time to get to this book. I always have felt I have had at least a couple of books inside of me, but I never thought of myself as a writer, so it just stayed a "feeling" for a long time. In my head, I was a coach, a mentor, a teacher, and a motivator. It's where I was happiest, and passing on knowledge and skills was my vehicle to that happiness. Helping someone to make a big enough breakthrough that they no longer needed me, and they could confidently assume the driver's seat in their life, was the best feeling ever.

One of my proudest moments was when I retired from the Beloit Fire Department, my shift said that, while they would miss my personality, the new leadership was the same, if not better. What that meant to me was that I had done a good enough job training my replacement that he was at least as good (he was way better than me), and my shift would be well taken care of and would continue to grow. You see, your real legacy isn't what you did while you were at work, it's what you left behind when you retired. If you left it as good or better than how you found it, then you can be proud of your legacy, and I must tell you, I am.

I have also always been an advocate for the underdog. Not really sure why I was that person, but I did not like bullies. I hated to watch people with talent just mailing it in because they were scared or under-equipped or worst of all, bullied. It was part of the reason that I finally got around to writing this—because I can only reach so many people individually, while I can get to a whole lot more with a book.

IAN GREGORY

• • • • • • • • •

There are a lot of people I want to thank. The truth is I have learned something from every person I have met, and this book will turn into a novel if I spend time thanking them all. You were all important to my growth and I thank you all. One person stood out, though, and that is my wife, Karen. This book would not have been written without her. I hit the jackpot when I married her. I don't just love her; I really like her. She's my favorite hang-out partner, favorite person to travel with, best person to run problems by...

I won't bore you with the list because it's really long, so I'll just say, "Thank You Babe, thank you so very much. I love you!" As for the rest of you, it's time to get to reading and get to work so that you can so much better enjoy your life as you learn to hit your *SWEET SPOT*!

The world is a dangerous and unfair place to inhabit. Everyone reading this knows that, yet we keep trying different ways to make it fair and equitable, and none of it works. So how do we find happiness in the midst of all this drama? How can we find ways to be joyful and productive and reignite our passion for life? Well, funny you should ask because the answer is the *SWEET SPOT*!

THE SWEET SPOT

The *SWEET SPOT* is the intersection of how you are wired, what your strengths and weaknesses are, and your ability to come up with a plan that you can use to make it all work for you. It's the answer to why you can be happy and excited when everyone around you is scared and fearful. It's the reason you can see a brighter future for you and your family while the media and the politicians tell us the sky is falling. It's the intersection of the best of you, tempered by the worst of you, and driven by the way your brain works best. The *SWEET SPOT* is the best *you* with more to come! So how does a nobody like me have all the answers for a somebody like you? Well, funny you should ask...

Chapter Two

Ian's Story

I was born in Hong Kong, yes, the Hong Kong that now belongs to China. It once was a colony of the British, and my father, being an officer in the British Army, was stationed there for three years, and I was born at the start of that tour. So, I lived for three years in Hong Kong, and I have absolutely no recollection of any of it. That came back to bite me when I thought I had a valuable piece of information that could make me as cool, or even cooler than the cool kids, but no one believed me. You see, I only had the story, no proof, and as we all know, kids can be cruel. I only let people know my birthplace when I am directly asked where I was born, and even today, you still hear the same hilarious jokes of how cheap things were that were made in Hong Kong, including me. So yeah, hilarious.

My father was a warrant officer in the British Army. He earned that distinction through experience and hard work. Unfortunately for him (and us), the British Army has a hierarchy, and warrant officers were the lowest of the low. Any young graduate of the military academies in England held rank over any warrant officer. What that meant to us was that the housing on the bases, for the officers, was decided by rank. You could move to a base and take any officer's house that you wanted if you outranked them. Because of that, we moved 12 times before we moved to America, and I was 12 when we made that move. Upheaval and change were a part of everyday life for us.

As if everyday life didn't have enough uncertainty and danger, picture this: I was a stick-thin child with a shock of red hair, covered in freckles, with ears that, while being prematurely adult-sized, stood straight out. I was also dumb enough to have a smart and irreverent mouth. I was a beacon of light to every bully I ever encountered, and trust me, there was a new bully at every school. I probably could have avoided most interactions with those bullies if I had learned how to filter my mouth, or even if I could have avoided standing up for the underdogs.

I didn't have the ability to do either. But I did learn a very valuable lesson very early on, and that is if you stand up to a bully or make life more difficult for a bully, they leave you alone.

Most bullies are lazy and don't want to work hard for things they used to get easily, so a well-placed punch to the nose or a well-aimed kick to the knee usually were enough to stop most fights. There were a few occasions that resulted in me taking a beating, but it never happened more than once, at least not to me, and I have learned many lessons since then about tactics, techniques, and ways to make a bully a friend, so it never was something that held me back.

• • • • ● • ● • • •

My father was gone every six months for six months. His job entailed keeping the big engines on the ships running optimally, and the fleet he was part of spent six months overseas, every other six months. Got that? Well, I didn't. My father was a stranger to me for a long time. I had to figure things out for myself. Most kids that were on base did as well. We were a real independent bunch of little smart alecks.

The hardest day for all of us was when the fathers came home and our moms told them most of what we thought we would get away with because we had been good for the last two days before they arrived. When I grew up, the saying was "children should be seen and not heard", and also adults on the base were allowed to kill their children, and I know this because it happened to me many, many, many times. At least that's how it felt.

When you are a military brat and you feel responsible for yourself, it makes you a people watcher and a behavior manipulator. I learned quickly how to make people feel good about themselves so that it was easier for me to get them to do things or get things for me. Your sense of fairness and morality gets a little twisted, and every decision is tempered with what's best for me?

The thing about normalcy and repetitiveness, both in people and situations, is that every child should be able to experience it. It gives them a chance to develop in a safe environment where most people know each other, and you get a chance to experience normal relationships with people who are always there and act the same all the time. I had no concept of relationship-building because we moved so often. Everything in my life was temporary, including most people.

IAN GREGORY

• • • • ● • ● • • •

We moved to America when I was 12. School was easy for me, and I was bored. It seemed everything I thought of doing broke some rule, and yet I did it anyway. Still struggling with relationships, I kept everyone at arm's length but the good part was, the name-calling went away. Turns out if you hang around people long enough, and have a smart mouth and a give and take mentality, you end up getting left alone, at least as far as name-calling goes.

My saving grace was that I was funny, apparently, and the kids thought a smart rebel was eventually ok with them. The teachers, not so much. I was always a kid that did not suffer fools gladly, and if you were a teacher and you were mailing it in, you and I were not getting along. The best teachers, at least the ones I remember fondly, all called me names. They said I was unmotivated, lazy, hard to get through to, and selfish. But along with that, they also said I was talented, that they believed in me, and that if I put in some work, there was little I couldn't do. I think for most people, the belief is the game changer. Someone that believes in you is always going to get more out of you than someone that is doing the job because they get paid to.

THE SWEET SPOT

• • • • • • • • • •

I had a very uninspired and commonplace three-year stint in the military. It is only worth mentioning because I met people from all over the United States that were in the service, and many people from all over the world that were not. While I was still trying to figure out me, I was exposed to a lot of different cultures and a lot of different ways of thinking that helped me to better understand people and their differences, as well as their commonalities.

Now, lest you think that was good for me, there was also this: while I was learning people, I noticed that most military people I met in the Navy were terrible with money. We were paid on a monthly basis and very few of the people I met could manage their money to make it last anywhere close to the thirty days required until the next paycheck. So, I recruited two people from my ship to be enforcers and collectors and started loaning out money.

We had over three hundred enlisted men on that ship, and I slowly built the business to become the one to come to when money was needed, and because I had two of the baddest people on the ship in my employ, we had very little competition, so money was never a problem for me in the service. It was way too easy to make it, but also way too easy to spend it.

I was constantly throwing parties at the base, and when we went overseas, you can bet that every port we hit, we were going to rent scooters and explore those ports to find the best places to party and meet girls. I had such a great time in the military from an exploration and party standpoint, but I hadn't really discovered my gifts. There was a lot to learn, and my immaturity got in the way of a lot of growth and the ability to use my gifts properly. I still hadn't met my mentor, or mentors, yet and it showed in a very average and mostly forgettable naval career.

And then sometimes you get lucky. The day I left the service and went home, there was an ad in the paper for a firefighter/paramedic. Now I knew enough about me to know that trying to do a regular 9-5 job was never going to work for this kid. I got bored easily and was always on the lookout for something exciting and different–usually things that society thought of as illegal. So, this was a chance at a job that would be different every day, and sometimes even scary. That appealed to me, and I filled out an application to become a firefighter/paramedic with the City of Beloit Fire Department, which is located at the bottom of the state of Wisconsin, right on the border with Illinois.

THE SWEET SPOT

At the time, I was working at the Holiday Inn of Beloit as a bartender, and I was raking in the money. If you don't know what to do and you have a way with people, you should seriously consider being a bartender. All you need is the guts to get them talking about themselves, and they will throw all kinds of money at you. High school reunions were the best! By two hours in, I had most people convinced that I had gone to school with them, and I was hooking people up and making sure the shy ones got noticed. I was making bank, and loving it. Then I got bad news. The Fire Department had rejected me for this round of hiring, and I was number one on the next up list.

Me being me, I wasn't interested in second best, so I scrapped the whole idea of the fire department. I called up a buddy from the military and talked him into riding our motorcycles down the East Coast, starting from Boston, where he lived, all the way to the Florida Keys. That was literally the extent of the plan and because I had to put in notice, we would leave in two weeks. I believe in divine intervention to this day, because two days before I left for Boston, the Fire Department called and said one of the applicants had flunked their physical and if I was still interested, I had the job. I wasn't looking forward to that phone call I had to make to my friend, but he was so cool about it, and so happy for me, it just felt right, and I accepted the job.

• • • • • • • • • •

Enlightenment and growth come to us in many ways, mostly in fits and starts, and usually with a lot of work that helps us gain insight. This was one of those moments where, when I look back, someone or something was looking over me. There was probably no one in the world that knew me and my buddy who thought that trip was going to end well, and yet it still took me a long time to realize how lucky I got with that phone call from the City of Beloit. There was no telling what kind of trouble we could have gotten into on the road together.

I had a thirty-year career with the Fire Service. Now thirty years with any organization is quite an accomplishment, but allow me a little bragging on myself because thirty years with an active fire department is waaaaaay different.

I was given great training in order to become a certified firefighter, and even better training to become a paramedic at the University of Wisconsin Hospital, which is world-renowned, and one of the best teaching hospitals in the U.S. The problem is, it doesn't matter how good the instruction is, it can never come close to what happens in real life.

As a firefighter and paramedic, I have been exposed to situations that most people couldn't even imagine, and which go beyond any training that is offered anywhere. I was the attending paramedic, meaning it was my call on patient treatments, on the scene of a kid who was unbuckled and hit another car; he was essentially decapitated as he went through the windshield, so it should have been an easy call to just respect and cover the body and wait for the coroner, but the kid's father drove past the scene, recognized his son's car, and was losing his mind as he struggled to come to terms with what he was seeing. He wanted to see his son's face, and he was out of control and getting ready to be arrested when I intervened and let him see his son.

I had no idea what I was doing–I didn't remember any lecture that came close to addressing a situation such as this. I was going on pure instinct as a dad myself, and I let him look. Heartbreaking doesn't begin to describe it as we watched him come to terms with what had happened to his son. It is something you never forget and never want to see again, but it also diffused everything. Grief replaced anger, and we were able to help him instead of fight with him.

IAN GREGORY

I was also first-in on an auto accident where the car had caught on fire, and there were two individuals that had not been able to escape, and were already dead when we arrived. The problem for us was that as a human body burns, the muscles shorten from the heat, as do various other parts of the body, and it looks like the people are still moving around. Civilians didn't have the training we had, and they thought movement meant there was still a chance to save a life, and they were frantically screaming at us to pull them from this fully engulfed car. We followed the proper protocols and put out the fire first while we listened to the crowd call us butchers and murderers and cowards. It was hard to listen to, and even harder to not defend ourselves. All part of the job, they said, but I looked, and I didn't find any of that in the job description.

And then there was the other side of the coin. We had a gentleman that always engaged us as he passed by our station. He either stopped to tell us a joke, or just yelled something unrepeatable as he passed by. His wife, every once in a while, would make us cookies or cakes and drop it off for us. A real nice family, and very supportive of the department. One day, we got a call for "man down". In emergency services "man down" means either someone unconscious or not breathing. It's our guy and from the color of his skin, he had been down for a while.

THE SWEET SPOT

We implement our protocol, which is CPR, IV, and all the drugs we can onboard in this particular situation. We are working our collective butts off, but not holding out much hope as, like I said earlier, every indication was he had been down for a while. We get him moved to the ambulance and one of the guys notices that our defibrillator is showing an electrical pattern. We stop CPR and that pattern becomes a pulse. As we pull into the hospital, his eyes are open and he's trying to speak to us, but you can't understand him as we put a tube down his throat to breathe for him. He continues to get better, and 2 weeks later, he is discharged and we have an emotional reunion. Plain and simple, it was a miracle. For all of you that don't believe in magic in this world, I can assure you, it exists, and if we look hard enough, it is all around us.

As I said earlier, something different on a daily basis was almost a requirement for me as I was easily bored, and the Beloit Fire Department took that to a whole new level. I was a paramedic and firefighter and saw people under some of the worst stress in their lives, and the ability to mitigate those situations became my hallmark as I could almost anticipate people in their actions. My observational skills and experience with the many personalities I had encountered really paid off.

IAN GREGORY

I don't tell you these stories to get you to feel sorry for my experiences or to elevate what I've done in any way. They are just to illustrate that I have seen people at their very best and at their very worst, and I have observed how much habit and learning have affected people's ability to navigate their way through a very difficult, demanding and sometimes scary and violent world.

• • • • • • • • • •

TAKE AWAY:

We are the result of our experiences, both good and bad. All too often, we are judged by those experiences, and usually it's the negative experiences that are highlighted, to the detriment of the person being judged. And yet, when I look back at my experiences, it's the negative ones that I learned the most from. It's the problem-solving that had to result from my poor choices that grew me, so I don't look back at my life and say certain things were good or bad. I use a different perspective in that I look back and ask myself: Did I grow from that experience or not?

Chapter Three
LIFELONG GROWTH

Growth occurs throughout life and you are a reflection of that experience. It's not the experiences themselves that reflect who you are, but how you grow from them. You get to decide from that experience how you will grow or not, whether you will move forward or be stopped. I realized that the decision is mine. For me, that's huge; I get to be final say in my life, and I want to protect that right forever.

Before I realized it, I had four children, which doesn't seem possible, but like most people, I didn't have a plan, and life happened quicker than I was ready for. I can't tell you how many people have said the same thing to me. Anyway, my children were all different in so many ways. Before the world had even started its indoctrination of my kids, I noticed that they reacted differently to stress, to rules, to the outdoors, and even to their parents.

I also noticed early on that different children were treated differently all throughout life, and for a variety of reasons. They seemed to be categorized in educational institutions by their ability to regurgitate information and take a test. The entire institution judged only the best test-takers as the most intelligent kids, and everyone else was less than. The winners were few, and the losers were many.

• • • • • • • • • •

I just never really got onboard with the way education was done. I always thought there had to be a better way; one, to get more people to understand that there are many forms of intelligence, and all of them are important in the real world, and two, to find a way to help those who weren't labeled as winners to understand and feel good about the gifts they *did* have, and to know that they, too, were every bit as intelligent as those "winners".

It bothered me that two of my children seemed to be wired for school, and it was even easy for them.

THE SWEET SPOT

That's because they listened and had good recall; they were considered to be in the smart-people group, while the other two were wired differently, and even though they put in much more work and study than the other two, always seemed to find themselves on the wrong side of the current educational system, and therefore were placed in the not-so-smart-people group. Talk about a system that grows more rebels than leaders, more dummies than geniuses, and more losers than winners. It just doesn't have to be that way.

A system should fit the needs of its participants, not the other way around. Why don't more kids get a chance at winning? How did "memorize and regurgitate" become the best way to judge a person's intelligence? When you see the kind of money that is being thrown around in this system, you start to realize what this really is all about, but I'm not here to denigrate a huge monolith. I'm here to deliver good news: the vast majority of people have a chance to be a winner in life, regardless of what their grades say, when they realize how they are wired and what are their strengths and weaknesses.

• • • • • • • • • •

TAKE AWAY:

IAN GREGORY

We all have our stories, in fact a lot of who we are and how we interact with the world is because of our stories, and yet, how many of us remember how far we really have come? We bend to the demands of the world, our work, our families, and our friends, and we slowly become something else, but we forget our contribution to that.

I meet way too many people who feel less than, who feel like they really don't measure up in the world, that are intimidated by rich people or academics with lots of letters behind their name or athletes, and they completely forget what they have learned and overcome themselves. All too often, we run from our stories, we don't think our stories are valuable or important enough to remember or repeat, and we slowly forget the essence of our brilliance.

I want you to remember who you really are, where you came from, and everything that you have overcome to get to this point. I want you to start living a conscious life, one where you recognize all of your accomplishments and your failures, so that when you take your rightful seat as the driver of your life, you will be the decision-maker for your future. You will take in all the information that you need, and you will have final say. It is possible, even in this crazy, blindingly fast-changing world, to be hap-

THE SWEET SPOT

py and content, but you have to find your *SWEET SPOT*.

Chapter Four
STRENGTHS

In today's world, I would be considered a nobody. I don't have a master's degree or a PhD, I'm not known outside of my sphere of influence, and I certainly don't have any credentials that would validate me as an expert, except for this: I KNOW HOW TO GROW PEOPLE. I know how to help people find their *SWEET SPOT* so they can grow and get better. I have been planting these seeds my entire adult life, and I have thousands of individuals who I have watched those seeds sprout and grow wings. I have even seen miracles in rebels and malcontents that only needed a chance.

You only need three things in order to succeed in my system:

THE SWEET SPOT

1. A need, not a want, but a *need* to change your life.

2. A working knowledge of how you're wired, and what your strengths and weaknesses are.

3. A plan.

That's it! I will give you the things to work on and you can take it from there. Is this a chance for everyone to be a winner in life? As they used to say on *Laugh-In*, "you bet your sweet bippy!"

It has taken me a long time to get to this point, but now everyone has a chance to find their *SWEET SPOT*. That intersection of how you are wired, what your strengths are, and what your weaknesses are is your *SWEET SPOT*. This book will show you how to get there, and is going to give every generation a chance to start strong and finish stronger because they will be happy in their *SWEET SPOT*.

• • • • ● • ● • • •

Let's start with strengths first. If you ask most people, they will say that a strength is something that you're good at, but that is not necessarily true. There are many people out there that are athletically gifted and love to play sports, but they don't like working on their sport. They don't like the tedium of practice and the repetition of the plays or the moves, they would rather just play. For those people, the sport is not a strength because they are not energized by the process of getting better, and sooner or later, they will be passed by someone with less talent but a real desire to improve, and their sport will then lose its luster, and growth will stop.

I'll give you another example–a personal example. When you work on a fire department, you are asked to write reports. It's a timeline of what happened and why, and it is needed in many cases because America is litigious, and going to court is just another part of the job. In order for a court case to reflect positively on an organization, it requires a well-written report. I was very good in that regard; I had a good command of the English language, and it was also important to me that I get the details right, and in the right order. The rest of the department, not so much.

We had a couple of cases go to court and the reports were so poorly written that the City ended up paying out money when they really were not at fault, they just couldn't prove it by the report. So anyway, they came to me and asked me to help the report writers get better.

THE SWEET SPOT

Now I had no desire to try and get anybody to do something they did not want to do, and these particular report writers most definitely did not want to get better. You see, my real strength was writing my own reports. I was energized by that—I felt good when I had written a story that was true and provable. But I was most certainly de-energized by trying to get someone else to have that same level of caring and competence that I had. If you didn't want to do something, I wasn't interested in the effort to change your mind, because I know how growing people works.

So, there we were, on opposite sides of a fight no one was going to win and I had no power on my side. I became a reluctant rebel. I started to become a thorn in the sides of the administrators who were ordering this debacle. I took report after report to them, tying up their day and asking inane questions about what the report writer was trying to say, and what word would be a substitute for nitwit or scum bucket. I simply turned it into a game that I was going to win, and I drove them insane while I played it. Finally, I "won" and they just gave up.

I didn't win any points with my administration, and I most certainly wasn't growing anything or anyone, including myself, during this particular time period, but I knew my strengths and I knew what this would do to me, so I had to change the outcome in order for me to start growing again.

When you find something that you are excited about, are willing to put in the effort to get better at, and you find that you are still energized at the end of the day, then you have found a strength. Think about why this is so important. If, at the end of the day, you go home to your family still energized by your day, they get the best of you, which they deserve. If you go home de-energized by what you do, then your family gets that too.

• • • • • • • • • •

Now there are a lot of really intelligent people out there who will be saying, that's great for those of us who are lucky enough to be working in jobs that appeal to our strengths, but some of you have to support families and the choice to work in your strengths isn't always available like it was for me. To them I say, hang around and keep reading. I will be addressing that very subject when we get to the section on plans. For now, it will be important for you to take a look at your life and see what it is that makes you feel great when you are doing it. What are the things in your life that you are willing to work

THE SWEET SPOT

at to get better just because you enjoy doing it? That, my friend, is a strength.

• • • • • • • • • •

TAKE AWAY:

Too many people in life forget about the best part of who they are because the emphasis is usually on shoring up your weaknesses. But when you think about it, how far can you really go in life if you are constantly working on the worst parts of you? If, on a daily basis, you are reminded that you are less than? What if you started working on the parts of you that you enjoy, that you feel good and even happy when you are working on that part of you? Now how far can you go? Work on your strengths more often and reap the benefits of that success. Start today, right now, and start remembering what makes you happy and what you are doing when you feel that happiness. It will go a long way to getting a handle on what your strengths really are.

Chapter Five

Weaknesses

It is also important for everyone to be aware of their weaknesses. Again, just like with strengths, it isn't about whether you are good at something or not, it is about how you feel while you are doing it, or how you feel about something after you've done it. If you feel de-energized, or disappointed and tired, then chances are that particular thing is a weakness.

When I was in high school, I was not a big fan of chemistry, physics, or science in general. The subjects didn't hold much value for me, and I thought it was just a weakness of mine. After I joined the fire service, I went back to college to pursue my degree, and found out that I really liked those subjects after all. It wasn't a weakness for me, it just didn't have any

THE SWEET SPOT

relevance for me at the time I was in high school. You see, those subjects are crucial to a long and safe career in the fire service. Knowing how things worked and how chemicals react to each other was a great thing to know when I was dealing with the kind of heat and situations that we ran into on a daily basis.

・・●●●・●●・・

We once had a call to a house that was exhibiting very light smoke, and nobody could figure out why. In the fire service we have a technique called positive pressure ventilation. It involves introducing large amounts of air into a space in order to clear that space out. It is a great technique when used in the proper context, meaning there is just smoke that needs to be cleared. It is not a great technique when you don't know the source of the smoke or what is causing it because that amount of air can take a small fire and make a raging inferno in no time flat.

So, anyway, my engine company pulls up to this house and the smoke is so light that no one entering is taking a hose, a tool, or any protective device in with them; it just seemed so safe and secure because the smoke was so light. But someone had turned on a positive pressure fan and it was facing the main entrance. I asked who had done this and why, and no one seemed to know. I simply unplugged it until we could find out why this house had this very light haze in it. We were then sent to the roof for further investigation. Apparently, while we were setting up for roof operations, someone turned that fan back on and set it in front of the main entrance once again. Within minutes, that house lit up like a Christmas parade. It looked fully engulfed in flames, so much, and so quickly, that we were pulled from the roof almost immediately.

As we were putting away the ladder, we heard glass break and saw a firefighter trying to exit through a kitchen window. The thing about kitchen windows is that they are usually higher windows than most and not good windows to exit from, especially for firefighters wearing protective equipment and SCBA's (Self Contained Breathing Apparatus). The firefighter was frantically trying to exit the window while flames were shooting out of the window as well. We made a quick pull and got the firefighter through the window safely, but lo and behold, another firefighter popped their head through that same window and they were screaming. The fire was reducing their protective gear to irrelevance, and they were in big trouble. Luckily, the firefighter I had with me that day was big and strong and we barely got that second firefighter through the window in time to save their life. Two saves, both needless. As it turns out, two others had been caught down the basement, had to make a run for it and barely made it out alive as well. So, because someone didn't understand the concept of positive pressure ventilation, we almost lost four firefighters. Talk about a weakness that can literally kill you.

In my line of work, you better know what you're doing, and the studying about all the things we can run into that can hurt or kill us is extensive and seemingly never ending. Too many of us were adrenaline jockeys with a weakness for study and reading—usually a deadly combination.

• • • • • • • • • •

Remember, a weakness is not something you are necessarily bad at, it's something that de-energizes you and makes you want to stay away from doing it simply because you don't like doing it.

Also, don't forget that your greatest strength can also be your greatest weakness. If you are competitive and want to do things at a higher level than is required, that is a personal decision and one to be applauded, but if you try to transfer that to someone else that isn't interested in going above and beyond, and just does what is necessary to keep their job, well then, your strength now becomes a weakness for somebody else, so you must be careful to not confuse strengths, weaknesses and the rules.

They can all be different things at different times, and they can most definitely affect different people differently. Got that? It means that everyone has their own strengths and weaknesses, and it shouldn't be assumed that everyone is the same.

A weakness must be shored up if it doesn't meet the standard of the organization that you work for, but that should be the only way that you should push someone in the direction of their weakness, to make sure that they meet the organization's standards. When they can meet or exceed those standards required, they should be pushed in the direction of their strengths.

Think about it: will you go further, work harder, and accomplish more if you are doing things that you like to do and really want to get better at, or would you rather have to face the worst you, on a daily basis, doing things that require so much effort from you to just make a standard? Pretty easy answer on that one, and yet every day, we run into organizations where they are just trying to beat square people into round holes, regardless of how much

THE SWEET SPOT

it is costing their personnel, their company, their bottom line, and their future. There is a much better way, as you will soon see, but first let's get to the real reason why this all matters.

• • • • • • • • • •

TAKE AWAY:

Don't run from your weaknesses; they give you a chance to learn about yourself and to work on change so you can grow and learn. But they are not where your future lies. People don't like to do things that de-energize them, because, well, it's de-energizing. You must be aware of what your organization requires from you and how you can meet those demands. All too often, people will take a job because it sounds great or it pays well, without any thought of if you are really wired for that job at all, or if it will only expose your weaknesses on a daily basis. Those things matter when the initial thrill of a job wears off, and you finally realize what it is that you'll be doing daily for maybe years in the future. So, while you can use the discipline of working on your weaknesses as motivation for being a better person, if you really want to be the very best you can be, you need to be working on your strengths, where the real you has a chance to be great.

Chapter Six
USING STRENGTHS AND WEAKNESSES FOR GROWTH

Everybody deserves a chance to be great. I have been a coach and trainer for almost fifty years now and there is one word that I have come to really dislike over the years. That word is "potential". To most people, potential means that you have the right stuff inside of you and all you have to do is get to it and voila, success! To me, potential means you haven't done anything yet. You see, it's not enough to have talent inside of you unless you are wired for that particular talent, meaning that you know and

THE SWEET SPOT

love that feeling inside of you to the point that you are willing to develop it.

I coached soccer for over twenty five years—everyone from the amazing five-year-olds to kids playing competitively in clubs to college kids. Way too many times I found myself in conversations with players and parents over how talented the player was, and yet they were far from realizing their potential in the sport. Over the years, I realized that if you were wired for what soccer requires, you put in the work and the reading to become proficient, and the talent that was inside of you developed. But no matter how much talent was inside of you, if your wiring didn't measure up, you just weren't going to dedicate yourself to developing what was inside, and you would eventually phase out of the game as the ones who were dedicated passed you by.

• • • ●• ● ● • • •

The same holds true for any talent that is within you. Whether you have an affinity for a sport or sports, English, math, science, politics, etc.; it doesn't matter. If something inside of you doesn't enjoy what you're doing, you will never reach the heights of someone who does enjoy it. And it's simply because they are wired for it and will develop it.

IAN GREGORY

We are all capable of many great things, but where do we go to develop ourselves? Not in schools because that would mean we would all be treated as individuals, which schools won't do because they don't think they have the time. It's not in the home because most homes don't understand the synergy between strengths, weaknesses, and how we are wired. It's not at work because they require rigidly defined roles from their employees. The only people who are being helped to develop themselves are those who either have a teacher or a coach, and even then, there are no guarantees because if the teacher/coach doesn't understand that same synergy, the same lack of development will show itself sooner or later for a myriad of reasons.

It is so important that you realize the difference between training and development. In training, you only need a coach to teach you how to do a particular sport or a job. You will be taught what is involved in doing the job and what part you must play in order for that job to be accomplished.

Development takes that so much further as it teaches you how to think while you are doing the job, so you aren't just relegated to doing the job, but you know it so well that you can fix anything that goes wrong, and maybe even anticipate future problems before they become actual problems. It means that

THE SWEET SPOT

you have learned the job so well that you might actually be able to teach someone else how to do the job. It also means someone is paying attention to your strengths, weaknesses, and your wiring. You simply have to understand how people are wired in order to help grow another human being.

• • • • ● • ● • • •

One of the best examples of the synergy between strengths, weaknesses, and wiring is quarterback Tom Brady. As of this writing, Tom was a quarterback on the Tampa Bay Buccaneers. He also played for most of his career with the New England Patriots. Tom has won more Super Bowls than any other quarterback, ever! You would think that someone with that kind of talent would have been taken first in the draft, but Tom wasn't. Tom Brady was the seventh quarterback drafted that year. Six guys, in the esteemed estimation of some of the best scouts in the country, were better than Tom and more deserving of a higher draft pick.

You see, most sports make their decisions, at the professional level off of stats and the experience of their scouts. What was evident was that nobody was looking at how the strengths, weaknesses, and wiring would impact those seven players. Mr. Brady passed them all by a mile to become, in most people's estimation, the greatest of all time (GOAT).

The sport I coached was soccer, which is a team game. In fact, it is one of the hardest sports to coach because there are eleven players on each team and there is no way to communicate with all eleven players at once, and the action is not controlled by coaches, refs, or fans, it is controlled by the players. So, it is a game that requires the players to be able to think for themselves and to control the game not just through their actions, but those of their teammates.

So, what if you have a talented player that just wants to dribble the ball through everyone and get a shot off? That individual loves to dribble and shoot, but not pass. No matter how talented a player is, they won't last long if they think they can play 1 vs 11 and the team will suffer in the interim. I have coached school teams and club teams, and I have even run an entire club for a few years, and I have had many occasions to interact with both parents and players in deciding what was best for the player and the club or school.

It is amazing to me how many parents are really just vicariously living through their kids, and whether they are suited for it or not, the parents want their child to be what they were not. It is a difficult conversation to have with these families when they are faced with an outsider who knows about the *SWEET SPOT*, and it is very apparent that the player is not team oriented, or isn't interested in putting in the work required to be good at soccer. I have told parents on many occasions that their player is wired for an individual sport rather than a team sport, and so far, no parents have come back and told me I'm wrong. It's because I watch for talent and wiring, and I watch for the weaknesses that will show up, and I make my determination based on what the player is showing and telling me.

All too often, coaches pick players by the talent that they see in the immediate, when they should be balancing out the strengths, weaknesses, and wiring of every kid they see. It isn't about that day of tryouts; it's about the future after tryouts. Some kids are there because their parents are pushing them in a certain direction; some kids are there because they think the reputation of the club will be enough to ensure their future; some even come to the tryout because their friends are trying out. None of those are enough for me to say yes to a kid. I want to see if they are first enjoying what they are doing; I want to see how well they get along with others; I want to see how they take direction and discipline. When I see a player that is exhausted and has given a great effort in the tryout, but they have this huge grin on their face and they are laughing and joking with their teammates, that player will get a higher consideration from me because I know they are acting out how they are wired, and any coach can work with that.

Talent alone is rarely enough, except maybe for the younger years when a little extra speed or natural ability is enough to make you stand out. The real test is how does a player react when faced with competition at or above what they are used to; do they go to excuses and complaining, or do they tighten their belt a notch and go to work?

• • • • ● • ● • • •

The same holds true for anything outside of sports as well. Schools are probably the best example of that. They are not set up to push children to realize their full potential; they are set up to continue to receive that government money. I know I'm going to get criticism from some people on this, but the truth is: schools are failing our children. I'm not going after teachers because I believe they can only be great if the rules allow it, and they don't. The push for government money has become so great that public schools have changed most of their curriculums to make sure that as many kids as possible pass the government tests so they can continue to receive that government money.

I coached college soccer for well over a decade, and none of those kids knew who they were or what their strengths and weaknesses were, and this was after twelve or so years in a system that was supposed to grow kids. We had alumni reunions every year, and I was blessed to be able to keep up with a lot of our players and see how they were doing. Of the hundreds of kids who came through our program, I only knew of one kid that was actually working in the area of his degree. Everyone else had just picked something to get a degree in because the college demanded it after your sophomore year. They had no idea of what they should be doing with the rest of their life, and didn't get it figured out until well after they had paid sometimes over $100 grand (in many cases it's much higher than that) for a degree that they were never going to use. To come out of high school with little to no knowledge about who you are or what your strengths and weaknesses are simply means you will bend to the will of whatever system is in place to do your thinking for you.

• • • • • • • • • •

TAKE AWAY:

The idea in life is to keep developing yourself to become a better human being, a more well-rounded person who knows who they are, be confident in that knowledge, and take a bigger picture view of life, knowing that others matter as much as you do, and that enjoying life is so much better than dreading it. To gain that edge in life, you will need to have knowledge of how you are wired upstairs in your brain, what your real strengths can do for you, and how you can overcome your weaknesses. It is imperative that you get to know the real you because you will realize that your strengths are huge compared to your weaknesses. It's just in this world, we have been conditioned to work on things that are not our strengths, and it has all too often stopped our growth, because only working on our weaknesses is like facing the worst part of ourselves, every day, and we will slowly disengage and find refuge in our mediocrity or at least, just do enough to not stand out negatively anymore. Do you really want that life?

Chapter Seven
Wiring and the Brain

Sitting on top of our shoulders is this box we call our head, and inside of it is the most amazing organ we have: the brain. Everyone's brain is different from everyone else's brain. It is what differentiates us from all other species and also what separates us from each other. It gives us our uniqueness–our specialness. There are no two brains exactly the same, because a brain is responsive to the life we've led and lead, and everyone's experience is at least a little bit different from everyone else's.

Now I have a background in medicine; I was a paramedic and firefighter for thirty years, so I know a little about the brain and how it works, but I sure don't know everything, just like everyone else in the world. I know some things about how science thinks they know how the brain works, and some of it I'm ok with, and I'm familiar with many of the terms used when talking about the brain, but here's the real truth: no one knows how this thing works, and as much as we'd like there to be people who have figured it all out, there isn't anyone.

Books are written about what we think is going on, and gush over scientists who can light up a certain portion of the brain in response to some stimuli that they have initiated, but they can't predict what the future will bring because of it, and they can't explain some of the weird things that can, and do happen to some people. Explain idiot savant to me. This is a person who, for all practical purposes, is consigned to live a life that requires at least another person to take care of them, because they can't take care of themselves, but at the same time have this unimaginable gift that just seems to be present inside of them. They can tell you what the weather was like on any day in history, they can do remarkably difficult math equations almost instantly, they can play the piano like a maestro, and yet no one can explain why, or even what, is going on. Why do two people come back from war with serious brain injuries, and yet if you rehab them exactly the same, one completely recovers and the other one wastes away to nothing and dies?

THE SWEET SPOT

The truth is that we are still in the infancy stage of figuring out the brain, and all its capabilities. For decades, we have heard that we only use 10 to maybe 15 percent of our brain, and yet how many of you ever questioned how they came up with that figure? When they do CAT scans, again using different stimuli on the brain, they can literally get most, if not all, of the brain to light up, but they don't know how to utilize that in any way or use it to predict any one person's future.

I'm not saying that we haven't come a long way since we have started studying the brain, but I am saying that we still have more questions unanswered than answered. So, in my experience, there are no real experts in this field, which makes me just as expert as the next person. My advice is based on what I know, what I've seen, and all the interactions I've had as a coach, a teacher, and a mentor. So here goes.

We are all wired differently. Some of it is innate, in that the wiring was always there, and some of it is from experience, how we deal, and have dealt, with life. The brain has plasticity, which means that it has the ability to change its activity in response to inside or outside stimuli by reorganizing its structure, functions, or connections. So, the brain can change, adapt, and overcome. If you are dedicated and intent on it, you can change the way you think, react, and problem solve through practice and intent.

• • • • • • • • • •

As a firefighter, we were expected to do the opposite of what normal human beings were doing, which was running away from a fire in complete panic. We were expected to size up the situation, protect life and property, and get that fire under control. There was only one path to that solution, and it was education and training. We had to learn everything we could about fire, what caused it, what fed it, what made it deadly, and what killed it. And then we had to train relentlessly, because there was so much to overcome psychologically.

Fire isn't just deadly because it's hot and produces smoke; everyone knows it's hot, and most everyone knows that smoke is deadly. It's the panic that ensues when you are actually confronted with a fire. When you can feel that heat starting to burn your skin, and that smoke is making you cough violently, and you now have to make decisions that you've probably never even considered. It's those decisions you've never thought about that overwhelm you. We train to rewire ourselves past the panic, we train to still be able to think while in the midst of chaos.

THE SWEET SPOT

Fire has changed on so many levels and we have had to keep up. There are so many more chemicals out there now, so many new and sophisticated plastics that have been invented that took fire to a whole new level in terms of how quickly it can kill and destroy. As if that weren't enough, the construction industry started building houses with 2x4's, which took the time we had to operate safely at a house fire and cut it at least in half.

The only response to those kinds of changes is training and development. You have to combine the two. Training teaches you how to respond, development teaches you to think while you respond. Mere training has never been enough, you must engage your brain.

So, what impact does how your brain is wired have on a daily basis? Well first, do you even realize how you're wired? Are you a people person? A behind-the-scenes person? A look-on-the-bright-side kind of person? A look-up-to-the-sky-to-see-if-it's-falling person? We all have certain tendencies that have been with us forever, and yet we don't even realize that we are like that.

I have friends that pretty much cover the spectrum when it comes to being wired differently. I have a friend that is not very social, will not speak unless spoken to, feels very uncomfortable in conversations with different points of view, and would much rather have a movie night alone than go out and interact with humans. I have another friend that cannot stand being alone, almost has to have the company of other humans around them. They are in constant need of feedback from everyone and have trouble making decisions on their own. They are both firefighters, very good in what they do, and yet, they are so completely different in how they act, interact, and problem solve.

What about how you learn? Can you get everything you need from a lecture? Do the words that people speak get through to you in such a way that you can actually duplicate what the speaker is trying to get across? Or, are you more like me and need to see it done, then get a chance to do it and practice it before you can say that you have actually learned something?

• • • • • • • • • •

There is an author by the name of Temple Grandin and she is autistic. By her own admission, Temple doesn't have a huge array of skills to offer the world, she is not interested in the world much outside of

THE SWEET SPOT

her own, she isn't the most comfortable around people in general, but she is wired for detail, almost fanatically so, and she has an affinity for animals to such a degree that she is the foremost authority, in the world, for the development of the serpentine ramp which has changed the entire cattle industry from the movement of the cattle to how they build slaughterhouses.

Her ability to see the world differently enabled her to tap into a more humane and efficient way of dealing with livestock that was revolutionary. She works it all out in her head first. She can see the finished product before anyone can sketch it or computerize it. She does it without thinking, almost reflexive. She is simply wired for it. And because she is tapped into that, and because she realizes how much different we all are, and most of all, because she realizes how different she is, Temple Grandin is a star. She has her own TED talk. You could go anywhere there are cattle people, and they will know her name. Oh, by the way, Temple is happy. She totally enjoys her life. Wouldn't that just be the best goal for us all, to totally enjoy our life?

• • • • • • • • • •

TAKE AWAY:

IAN GREGORY

I have been teaching for a long time that the only thing stopping you is *you*, but for you, what does that really mean? The brain is plastic and trainable, but from a very young age, it is usually someone else that is doing the training and the growing, and after a while, we come to depend on someone else doing that training and growing for us, and we are not ready for the independence that real life demands of us.

Chapter Eight
THE NEED TO CHANGE

I'm here to tell you that are going to have to get to know yourself a whole lot better than you do now. I am fascinated by how different everybody is from each other. Over the years, it has been so much fun watching people become aware of their wiring, their interactions, and so forth, and even more fun helping people make changes that work for them and grow them. You see, it's not just a possibility that you can change, it's a guarantee.

Like I said before, you just need three things:

1. A need, not a want, but a *need* to change your current life.

2. A working knowledge of your wiring, your

strengths, and your weaknesses.

3. A plan.

That's it. Three things that can change your life for the better, forever. I'm doing all the heavy lifting here with the information contained in this book, so what's your role? Your role is the <u>need</u> and the plan. This will be intensely personal as you realize only *you* can grow a better you; everyone else is just a helper. If you are dissatisfied with the way things are going, or you feel that you are stagnating or even regressing–if you feel like there is more to you that is not showing, or you think you have more to offer, you have the beginnings of a need: that feeling that you want to see what you really have inside. If that feeling is real, if you have a need to be brave and not be afraid to find out who you really are, then keep reading. You're going to see a way to change your life for the better. For the rest of you, don't bother.

I'm not saying that to be a jerk, I'm saying that because without the need, I'm going to open you to inner conflict and dissatisfaction, and it will make your life worse, not better. If you have ever made a New Year's Eve resolution, you know the one: quit smoking, lose weight, go to school, etc., then you already know the odds of following through on your wants and desires. They are slim to none. It is hard to change you, because you have put so much work into the current you. All your habits that you put in place, all the mannerisms, all the strategies, all the daily affirmations that have resulted in the current you are going to get in the way of the future you. All of the old you doesn't go away because you desire it to, or you *really* want it to.

You have probably spent decades on the current you, and whether it is working well for you or not, this is the result, and it's pretty ingrained and not easily changed. You really have to have a need, a deep-seated reason, that keeps bugging you and says, I can do better. I need to do better. And that voice needs to be strong, vibrant, constant, and consistent. You are about to face you, and that's not always pretty. You ready to make that change? Keep reading!

• • • ● • ● • • •

TAKE AWAY:

When you leave your home and go out into the real world, you should be ready right? You should know who you are, how your brain is wired, what your strengths and weaknesses are, and how to make all that work for you. The real truth is: very few of us are at that level when we leave the nest. We have had a lifetime of being told what to do, and in many instances what to think, and we are not even independent learners when we leave; we are dependent on others for help.

I'm not trying to get you to think that you don't need other people in your life—people enrich us; they grow us; they make life fascinating and compelling, but they should never be the final say in your life. A great example are doctors. How many of you go to a doctor and just do whatever the doctor says? I would guess many, if not most. I realize that I pay doctors for information and that their job is to get me to totally understand what is going on so that I can make the decision for myself, because I'm final say. Get it? If a doctor can't explain to you what is going on so that you can fully understand it and make a decision, then you need to find a doctor that can. That is called taking responsibility for your own life, and I think all too often we give up that duty because we have been conditioned to allow others to decide and act for us instead of us being the driver of our own bus.

Your brain is extraordinary and if you use it for what it was intended, you can be extraordinary as well. Let's get started working on your plan!

Chapter Nine
The Plan

You need a plan to move forward. I know, I'm about to lose a lot of you that have tried "plans" in the past and weren't able to get to the end, but don't give up, this plan is different. This plan is about you–not me–this plan is about discovery and hope–not rules and rigidity. This plan is about growth. Yours. Lots of it. It's about that little voice that keeps telling you that you can and should be better but keeps getting drowned out by the noise of work, home, kids, obligations and in general, life. I want that little voice to have more say in your life. I want it to be the catalyst for growth.

The best part about your upcoming plan is that it works in conjunction with your life, not against it.

Not that you won't have homework; you will. It's just that the homework is really just doing things that you have always done, but doing them a little bit differently. If we are serious about our growth and our future, then we have to learn to get to know ourselves and more importantly, trust ourselves!

Also, while I'm talking about the plan, I'm going to be jumping back and forth between the plan, the brain, and examples. I know that will irritate some of you because your wiring likes things in order by number, and please don't deviate (I realize how different we all are), but I also know plans in place are not plans completed. Many things can, and will, get in the way of you completing what you want and growing yourself. All too often, those plans never come to fruition because we don't understand that we sabotage ourselves, not intentionally, but because we have put habits in place that at one time, worked for us, but now are working against us, yet we continue them simply because they are habits that we are familiar with, and we don't take the time to really examine ourselves and see if we can make our lives better and grow ourselves at the same time.

• • • • • • • • •

THE SWEET SPOT

I really want your plan to work, and because every single person in this world is different, there is no one plan that will accommodate that, so I can't set down your rules for you or set timelines for you–that is your input. As you understand more and more how your brain works and can see ways that will work for you, you will create the best plan possible for you, and only you, and that is my goal. So, I will be switching back and forth a bit for the next few pages because the understanding of it is as important as the plan itself. Please bear with me and keep reading as you will see the understanding will be the greatest addition to your success.

Ready? Get out a piece of paper and write on it who you are–everything that you are, and don't hold back. Get as much of you down on paper as possible. Don't be afraid to ask others what they think to help you round out the list more fully. So, at the end, it should look something like this: husband/wife, father/mother, friend, teacher, golfer, reader, tv watcher, liar, writer, cheater, dancer, singer, game player, procrastinator, comedian, egotist, finisher, competitor and so on.

You'll notice that the list is not designed to just promote the best things about you, but if you are to have an honest discourse about who you are and where you would like to be, you have to be honest about the behaviors you exhibit and the stands you take. When that list is complete, separate it into two columns. Things that you think are positive and things you consider to be negative.

Also, when you write those two lists, make sure you rank each list in importance as well. For instance, if you value being a dad or mom over being a friend, make the list reflect that by placing it above friend. It is important that you do this from your point of view. Ultimately, growth is extremely personal, so make this your decision.

All too often, we end up being who we are, not by our own decisions, but by decisions made for us by others. All those voices that try to influence us with their wisdom from when we are extremely young–parents, friends, neighbors, teachers, schoolmates, the media, professors, peers, counselors, etc.–they all have their own version of what they think is best for us, and rarely do any of them stop and say: how are you and how are you feeling? So, now I'm asking.

Is this version of you the best version? Is there anything nagging at you that you would need to change? More importantly, which version do you want? Many people can get you to try the newest diet or fad or the newest psychological tip, but if you are not in complete alignment and agreement with any

THE SWEET SPOT

of it, then none of it will take and you will return to the world that you have created where, whether it is a great world or not, you know the routine, and we all take comfort in our routines.

• • • • ● • ● • • •

So how do you change the current version of you? First, realize that only *you* can. Influencers can help, as can mentors and anyone else you trust, but they can't do the work for you, and the work is the only thing that will make the changes stick. Now the real trick is to not make it seem or feel like work, because, for some reason, we associate work negatively, as though work is a bad word.

Think about it, when you are engaged in something and you're enjoying it, you'll say something like, "I was having so much fun, it didn't seem like work." Yeah, we are weird like that. You are still working, but because you're enjoying it, you can't name it something negative, so it can't be work right?

Let's go back to the lists you created. Some things are going to go on only one of the lists whether it is positive or negative, some are going to go on both, for example, I have an ability to concentrate when I'm doing something that I like, which sounds like a positive until someone wants to talk to me while I'm concentrating–then it's negative. Like they say, sometimes your greatest strength is your greatest weakness.

Now here is what's most important with these lists. You must define what you have personally contributed to each designation that you make. So, for example, you can be a mom or dad, which is just a result until you add to it what your contribution was, and now you can be loving-mom, and yet impatient-mom. You can be fun-dad, and still be demanding-dad. See the difference? It's not enough for you to just say what you are, you must add your contributions to that to further define the kind of person you are. So, can you be a hateful niece, a loving sister, a difficult child and a loved-by-all student? Of course you can.

We are trying to get to who you really are and get you to start facing the reality that you are, and can be, many different things to many different people. If change is needed (not wanted or hoped for, but *needed*), there must be obvious reasons why the change is needed, and seeing yourself for who you really are is one of the early catalysts to start that change.

THE SWEET SPOT

• • • • ● • ● • • •

If you still are struggling with this part of it, LIA Leadership In Action offers a 360-Degree Assessment. We don't use DISC or Briggs-Meyers, or any of the many other self-assessments that are out there. I'm not looking to put any of them down, but for the most part they are going off how you feel about yourself on any particular day, and you have the final say. We use the 360-Degree Assessment because it involves people whose judgment you trust, who have seen you over a long-ish period of time and have seen at your best and your worst. While we are busy putting on our masks for the world, trying to get the world to see us in the best light possible, these people aren't fooled. They know you and have been dealing with the real you for a long time now, and they know what's really up.

The 360-Degree Assessment is a very emotional experience because you, maybe for the first time, are opening up and allowing someone else to help you shape a better you by exposing the best and the worst of you from their perspective. Not everyone buys in at first, but they all eventually acknowledge that they may not be perfect. The longest we have ever had to wait was three weeks.

IAN GREGORY

We were teaching a class for an EMS office full of trainers and had this one guy who was the office manager, and also a teacher. He was very good at what he did, but he came across as arrogant–like no one could come up with a better solution than he did. When his 360 came back and he was called out for how he treated people, he was livid. How dare they treat him like this, how dare they say anything to someone like him? See? Arrogance, right? So, I told him to not make any decisions. Just let it marinate for a while, let the best of you try to reconcile the worst of you without taking any retribution against those who were just trying to help.

Sure enough, three weeks later, I get a call from him. "They're right," he says, just like that. I was dumbfounded. "What made you decide that?" I asked. He said he knew it right away, but felt like he had given so much to them that he felt like they shouldn't have the right to beat him up like that. But then, the good part of him realized that he could actually be holding some of them back by what they were describing, and he couldn't live with that. I wrote that date down, because to me it was profound.

When we were in the last day of class, we asked if things had changed around the office, and every single person said yes, it had changed, and for the better, and they even said they could name the day

THE SWEET SPOT

that it all changed. You have already guessed it was the day that I had written down, and to us here at LIA Leadership In Action, it just proved how life-changing and life-affirming these 360's could be.

Anyway, whether you take the 360 or not, you have your list. That important list of the good and the bad should be looked at on a daily basis. During this time, feel free to add to the list as you rethink the real you and where you might be headed. Also, during this time, I don't want you to feel the pressure of immediate change that so many people who are starting on a journey like this feel. This is about change–real, life affirming change that won't happen overnight, and there is no allotted time period for it. The rules are different for everybody because everybody is different. It's a process that should be respected by taking your time, by asking tough questions, and by really asking yourself, "Will it be a better life if I pursue a better me?"

If you have completed your lists of positive and negative and really put some thought into it, congratulations! Most people in life never get to this stage. They just play out the string, hoping that something comes along (like a lottery ticket), that will solve all of their problems and get them on the right road. Well, here's the rub. Documentary after documentary has shown that lottery winners, even the ones who win over a million, are usually broke within a year because they never changed who they were, and because of it, they had no skills in handling or growing their money; what they wanted had never been reconciled with what they needed, and money has a habit of leaving, and fast, when it's not respected.

Sorry to burst your bubble in regard to winning the big horse race, or the lottery, or picking the right cryptocurrency, but there is a better way. How about we bet on you, the better you? How about we find out what your real strengths and weaknesses are, figure out your wiring, and come up with a plan to leverage all of that–a plan that takes advantage of what you do well and naturally, and figure out a new path to success?

Remember, when you think about it, people have been trying to control you since you were a toddler. Parents teach you how they think you should act and think, schools most definitely try to teach you how to act and think, your job and the workplace tell you how to act and think, even the news and entertainment folks all get their two cents in on how you should act and think. So, when do you get to just stop and think for yourself?

THE SWEET SPOT

When is it ok to compare what your strengths and weaknesses are and how you are wired with what others are saying, so you can decide for yourself how you want to respond to the world around you? Whether their thoughts and opinions will really work for you, or do you just parrot back to the world what your favorite newscaster or entertainment opinion/fact finder is telling you to say? We seem to be losing our ability to have a conversation where people have varying and sometimes strong viewpoints on how they perceive the world. If you cannot hold a conversation with anyone who holds a different viewpoint, imagine how boring conversations will be. You already know what the other person is going to say, ad nauseum, and nothing is furthered with those kinds of conversations because the brain doesn't need to be engaged to have them. And what does it say about you that you won't allow another point of view to muddy the waters?

This life is messy and unpredictable, and it most definitely is not fair, so why would you face it with an under-educated and under-utilized mind and brain? If we are to find the success that we so richly deserve, we must think our way through this world, not react our way through it. It is not the same world it was when I was a young-un, and it won't stay the same world that it is right now. If you go through this process and start engaging that wonderful brain of yours on any kind of a regular basis, you are going to be surprised and excited about the changes that you can make to become a better you.

• • • • • • • • • •

I have seen miracles when people start tapping into who they really are on a regular basis. I met a young man that had recent prison time in his past, and he was dating my niece, so I wanted to, as a caring and loving uncle (nosy and curious), find out what was what. So, I engaged this young man in conversation and in that conversation, he was very open and honest about the mistakes that he had made leading up to his incarceration, yet he felt like he had a lot of skills, not just with machinery but with people as well, he just hadn't found himself yet.

As a leadership trainer and developer, I hear this a lot, so I asked him if he was interested in a mentor who could help him with better decision-making and how to take advantage of these skills he thought he had. He didn't hesitate and was grateful that someone would offer him a chance, especially so soon after his "problems." Fast forward only five years, and he is the Director of Corporate Operations for Doumak, the second largest marshmallow maker in the world, in line to become Vice President.

The only differences between then and now are that he has been educated on how his brain works, what his strengths and weaknesses are, and how that can translate into a plan for the future. He planned all this, not me. He put in the work that was necessary to keep moving up, and he kept asking the questions about problem-solving that led to new ways of doing things and new ways of communicating. He really did have some very marketable skills, both with machinery and people, he just needed a plan to take advantage of that, which I was grateful to be a small part of.

The best part of this whole thing is that people ultimately have to do it for themselves, and they can see results and success and know that it is because they were willing to work on themselves, willing to put some time in to develop their brain, and willing to prepare for future success.

• • • ● • ● • • •

So back to your lists. Take a good look at them and look at the contributions you made to both. It was your contributions that made that list personal, made it yours. The things that you did on a regular basis not only programmed your brain to react and think a certain way, but it programmed how you react to the world.

You see, habits can be a great thing for us, they can ensure that we do a great job, day after day, that we're the person you can count on. They can also be a terrible thing for us, as again, if you've trained yourself to do less, or cut corners, or do things just so you can say they are done, well, people see that behavior as well. You see, the bottom line about habits is that they make us reactive.

When you allow yourself to repeat behaviors, and for whatever reason, you think those behaviors will work for you, then every time those situations present themselves, you will react the same way, basically because you have trained yourself to; that's why I wanted you to look and see what you contributed to that. What behaviors were you working on that resulted in you automatically yelling back at someone who yells at you, what was the end goal that resulted in you writing down that you're fearful or angry or lazy?

Sometimes we really need to take a look at why we react to the world the way we do. We need reasons why we do certain things so that we can come up

THE SWEET SPOT

with a plan to change some of those things so that our world will get better. For instance, your relationships with various people are a result of what those people say, how they act, and how they treat you, and also the result of what you say, how you act and how you treat them.

You look at some toxic relationships and wonder how in the world those people stay in any kind of relationship when they are so mean to each other, and yet the truth is, they have learned that behavior. The dance that they are doing has been done so many times that neither side is fully aware of either their, or the other's behavior. Again, that is what habits can do for us and to us–we continue relationships that are bad because we are so used to that habitual dance.

It's those habits that you should be most interested in, or more to the point, the behaviors that led to those habits that you should be interested in, because it is through those behaviors that you will now have the ability to change any and all of the habits that you have acquired. You did this; you can fix it!

• • • • • • • • • •

Now up in your brain, we have these things called neural pathways. These pathways are how we send signals from one part of the brain to another. If the signal you want sent is new, something you haven't done before or are not sure of, the pathway is slender, weak, and sometimes inconsistent. Like when someone changes their mind a lot on something, it's because of a temporary or weak pathway. Now that sounds like that could be bad for you, but remember, no habits have been ingrained yet, so you are actually operating on your brain, thinking your way through something, which can be a good thing, especially for a brain that doesn't get a lot of work. We are still operating in the conscious mind and questioning things, and so while it may appear that the person is waffling or unsure of themselves, they are still working on what habit will result from this, or if it is even worth a habit for this particular issue.

Every signal sent through that same pathway strengthens it, makes it larger and easier to navigate through. Why is this important? Ever been to someone's house that has siblings in it, and they are constantly at each other's throats? After a while, you think you're in the twilight zone. These are family members, and they seem to hate each other. But as you watch, you realize they are not really mad at each other, that the terrible things they say to each other don't have the same effect on them as they do

THE SWEET SPOT

on you. To you this is new; to them this is habitual. Somewhere, probably way back, undesirable behaviors and mean words became part of the conversation, and nobody stopped it. Also, nobody got physically hurt, so they continued. As the dance was daily, so were the behaviors and the words. Over time, the neural pathways widened, strengthened, and habits were formed. Any word a certain sibling said set off a chain reaction that if you were really listening, you would recognize as a pre-programmed result. They weren't in relationship with each other, they were in habit with each other. If you were to confront them about their boorish behavior, they would probably look at you surprised that you thought they didn't like each other. Their dance was so orchestrated and normal to them, they didn't even listen to themselves anymore.

Humans organize their lives around these neural pathways and habits. These neural pathways and habits take the work of thinking out of the equation, and allow us to mostly go through our days on autopilot. What we don't do is stop and ask ourselves if the habits we have put into operation are really taking advantage of the gifts and talents that we all have within us.

Think about it, without habits, we would have to think our way through our world and our days. But what if thinking was our way out of this which we have created? What if we looked at things differently, from a more objective you and what is best for your viewpoint, rather than a subjective view of what everyone else thinks we should be and should be doing. I think we would all be happier and more successful if we were allowed to create our own box, that works best for us, instead of the box that everyone else wants to create for us, that works best for them.

So, we can use the power of our neural pathways, the same power that you used to create the habits you currently have, to create new habits and new ways of interacting with the world. These neural pathways are built, strengthened, and thickened by use. The more you use them, the stronger they get until they become habits, which is our autopilot system, right?

Here's the secret about those neural pathways that you would think should be obvious, but we rarely act on it: the less you use them, the weaker they become. And, if you can find a substitute behavior, then every time you use that new behavior, you weaken the old, and strengthen the new. It's just that easy. Well, it seems that easy until you have to consciously use the new behavior, then you find out how strong the habits you have put in place are.

THE SWEET SPOT

• • • • • • • • • •

TAKE AWAY:

It is estimated that acting habitually is between 45% to 90% of our behavior; that between half and all our behavior is reactive, not thought through. We did that to ourselves as we repeated behaviors for just over two months. That's right, it takes 66 days to make a behavior habitual. I know many of you thought it was just 21 days, but the caveat to that is that you must keep that 21 days going for an additional couple of months for that habit to become your go to, reactive behavior. So, the new research, coming from UCL Epidemiology and Public Health researcher Phillippa Lally in London, England, is 66 days.

Whatever the final number, it really is irrelevant. Everyone is different from everyone else, so I'm sure some people can make behaviors habitual in very short order, while others may take a lot longer to achieve the same result. What is clear is that habits are the result of repeating behaviors over time until they become our learned way of dealing with the world reactively. While you are using your habits, you are not thinking your way through life, you are reacting your way through it.

The good news is that you can fundamentally change how you deal with the world in a very short period of time. You can start repeating behaviors that work for the special and unique you, and you don't need anyone else to get that process started–just your brain.

Chapter Ten
Bringing The Plan To Life

Ok! Ok! Back to the lists, for real this time. Hopefully, you have been adding to the list all along as you are reading. The more detail you can list about your contribution, the better you can plan your new you. Let's look at how you can do that.

Say you listed yourself as "dad", but you thought about it and realized that you are different dads during the week, so you listed something like this: happy dad, angry dad, frustrated dad, proud dad, caring dad, disengaged dad, etc. All of those different dads are because of your contribution, right? In order for you to move from proud dad to angry dad, it required a contribution from you–you made that jump–mostly through reaction (habit) to a particular stimulus, and you changed to a different dad.

Most of the time, we justify that contribution by blaming the situation or the other person, and we forget our role in it. Did we have to make that change? Could we have decided to not react angrily? Of course you could, but you were up against a very strong force in the universe–the force of habit–you made that choice habitually, with no thought of yourself, the other person, or the consequences. You made that transition seamlessly, and in the blink of an eye, you went from proud dad to angry dad.

All too often people will take on the whole "dad" thing, and say, "I want to be a better dad" which is such a general statement, and what you will find is there is so much to that, as evidenced by the many different dads listed above, and so much to take apart and deconstruct that it very quickly becomes overwhelming, and like most New Year's resolutions, disappears from your life. Let's start with a challenge and go for success: First pick a specific dad, I'm going for angry dad, and then pick a place that you get mad, for instance home, work or church. I choose home. This is where you engage your brain and start the process of the new you.

THE SWEET SPOT

·•·•**·**•·•·

Thinking about what is bothering you and how you can overcome it is problem solving, and it is the best way to engage and strengthen the mind while growing your brain. It is the very antithesis of habit and should be encouraged on a daily basis. At home, after much thought, you realize your 13-year-old son sets you off because he takes forever to get to the point, and you feel like you're jumping from rabbit hole to rabbit hole as you try to keep up with his endless ramblings with seemingly no point to any of it. Not only rambling, but he does it the second you walk in the door from work, and you haven't even decompressed yet. Perfect place to start.

You realize, at least at some level, that you are pushing your son away, that he is getting less willing to engage with you, and you can literally see the relationship slipping. You must come up with a plan to make that relationship whole and happy again, wouldn't you agree?

Start asking questions like, "What is my role in this? Was I in a good mood when we sat down? Was I interrupted while doing something else? What was my son looking for when he engaged me?" As you continue to ask more and more questions, what will be revealed is the dance that you are doing is habitual. You will start to see that this dance has been done many times before, and you both are acting out of habit and reacting, rather than thinking your way through a new way of doing things.

Keep asking why and you may realize that your son is just looking for your approval and picking the wrong time or way to ask for it. You may realize that you really do love that kid, but he's asking for the best of you when you're in the worst frame of mind. If you put in enough thought, you may even realize that it isn't the relationship that's the problem; it may just be the circumstances, and if you just had 15 minutes to work out or talk things over with your significant other, or even if you just took your child for a walk and let him talk for the entire 15 minutes, then your anger would dissipate, while at the same time, you would probably be meeting a need in your child. Now if it were me, I would go for the double win.

I try to look at both sides in a relationship and figure out if both sides can grow from it. So, in addition to taking care of myself and instituting new habits for the new me, I would hope I would recognize that my 13-year-old son has an under-developed brain, in that he has little to no experience in, well, anything. So, for me, I would schedule time with my child on a regular basis, and we would play games or solve problems, because those are two of the best things you can do to engage and grow a brain.

While we are problem solving, I would do everything I could to allow my son to do most of the problem solving because he will benefit most from that, but I must also mention this: I will beat him at every game, every time, until he learns to beat me on his own. I will never rub it in that I won and he lost, and I will always explain any strategy or thought process that enabled me to win, because I'm interested in his growth. So, I will ask him to use me as his guide to getting better, in that while he may not beat me for a while, I'm his barometer, his gauge for how he is progressing, and the measurement will tell you that he is growing or slacking. It will also give you experience in patience, practice, growth and handling your emotions.

You see, when I try to grow people, I have high standards, and I expect to grow warriors, not just human beings. When I say warriors, I mean people who think their way through life, not react their way through it. At the end of this book, I'll better define what a warrior is and why it is so important to start training ourselves and our family as warriors because you really can think your way to a better you and a better world.

IAN GREGORY

• • • ● • ● • • •

In the example of the 13-year-old, let me ask you, how much did your life change? You thought about something, you got as much time as you needed to think and come up with a plan, and you implemented that plan. Do you think that relationship would change if you figured out how not to get mad, and you learned how to grow that child's brain? Of course it would, and it's really just that easy. It's the difference between living an unexamined life versus a thoughtful life. We really do have all the tools necessary to solve most, if not all, of our problems, but for some reason we see problems as negatives, as work, as things to get out of or not be bothered by, when in reality, they are just what you need for growth.

Now, you're feeling better about yourself, you took a small slice of your life and you made it better, and now you want to tackle more of the bad you so you can even be a better person, but you would be making the worst mistake. This is where we subconsciously, or even unconsciously, sabotage ourselves.

Let me explain. It is not a bad idea to work on yourself and make yourself a better person, but let's remember what we are trying to accomplish long-term. It is the best you that can possibly be right? In order for you to take it as far as you can go, you have to find a way to work in your strengths. Remember, while you are working on your weaknesses, you are facing the worst of you, the part of you that you have always struggled with, and it's a daily grind to overcome that, so only do it long enough for you to hit the standard that you have set for yourself. Meanwhile, pick a strength that you listed and would like to work on.

It's also important for you to be working in areas of your life that you enjoy, that you feel good about while you do it. That alone can be enough for you to keep working on your weaknesses because you know there is an endpoint to that. You only have to hit a standard, while with your strengths, you can go as far as you want to; the sky is really the limit, and you get to enjoy your life doing what you want and what you enjoy. For me, that's golf.

I love golf and everything it takes to play golf. I like talking about it, practicing, playing on my own, playing with friends, playing competitively, etc. I just love golf. Now, while I'm working on my problem issues, I'm also working on my golf game. It's the balance that I need to be able to confront the worst of me while I work on the joy in me. And because I am now more connected to what's going on, and no longer living an unexamined life, I don't get too low while working on my problem areas, and I don't get too high working on my strengths. See the difference? An unexamined life just feels like you're going from crisis to crisis, and the anxiety you feel is because you aren't growing a better you, you're just waiting on the next crisis and hoping you can find a way to get through it.

• • • • • • • • • •

An examined life will help you realize that while you are working on the best and worst of you, you are also growing that problem-solving part of your brain and the "I can do this" part of your brain, and these so-called crises will diminish in stature because you're a better problem solver, and not so easily knocked around by life's problems anymore. We must learn that while we are working on the worst of us, we are utilizing and growing our brain more than at any other time in our life. The brain engages when we step outside of our habits, have to problem solve, and deal with the seemingly endless problems of the world that we feel so responsible to solve.

An examined life helps us to let go of the anxiety of problems because they are our road to growth, and it also helps us to enjoy the feeling of happiness we feel when we are working in our strengths. Life is no more than a process of growth that hopefully never stops. You can best enjoy it when you realize what is really going on and how much you have already grown.

I would like to ask you a question. When was the last time you celebrated how far you have really come? You can go back as far as you want, but at one point, you couldn't tie your shoes, couldn't speak the language, had no concept of math, manners, relationships, or bills. Now look at you. All those things overcome, second nature to you now, and you take it all for granted. You can better learn to celebrate the wins, and even the losses, when you live an examined life, because even in the losses, you learned something, even if it was what not to do.

The examined life will allow you to quickly see where and how much you are out of balance, and will find ways to re-establish that balance, while celebrating how far you have come to be able to do that. It certainly helps if your work allows you to work in your strengths for much of the day because that feeling of accomplishment will follow you home and your family will get the best version of you as they rightly deserve, but also, people notice when you are enjoying yourself and becoming a better worker.

Now, I also get it, we don't always get our way, and sometimes we have to work at a job that we don't necessarily like in order to feed our family and pay our bills, and that family most certainly is not getting the best you in any kind of way, so now what? Well, most of your work is done for you. You know that you are going to experience brain growth because you are going to turn your attention to solving the problems at work, you are going to try to find ways to make your strengths work for you in either the relationships or the processes at work, and you are going to ensure that while you may not find joy in the daily grind, you are not going to be run over or plowed under by the attitudes that you used to bring in with you–that you are going to utilize that brain and at least find a way to make things better.

Meanwhile, you are going to look for that balance outside of work. Maybe it's a walk with your significant other, maybe it's exercise, maybe it's gardening (it would never be gardening for me), but it doesn't matter what it is, as long as it's something you enjoy doing. It's the balance that you need to find peace and contentment.

THE SWEET SPOT

Is any of this getting through? We make life more complicated than it is. We overreact to problems and we underreact to joy. We are letting technology get in the way of relationships, and all too often we are letting technology *be* our relationships, and it is STOPPING OUR GROWTH! Yes, I'm shouting because it is that important. It is through our relationships that we grow, love, learn, and live, and it is relationships that make all the other stuff palatable. Examine your life, get to know the real you with your strengths and weaknesses, use that to plan your future, and watch the magic happen.

• • • ● • ● • • •

TAKE AWAY:

Abraham Lincoln said that if you have a plan, you are already halfway to your goal. You have to put some thought into your plan, you have to know what you want to have happen with this plan, and you have to be acutely aware of the need that is driving that plan. The need for it is what will keep you going when others will stop or disengage. This plan will be the best for you because it will be you that lays out the steps, because only you know the real you, and only you know what is really best for you. As good old Abe said: you are already halfway home with a plan.

If you are ever going to realize your full potential, sooner or later, you are going to have to learn to trust yourself—you are going to have to be comfortable with who you are and how you interact with the world. You see, the world sees the masks we put on and they trust us less because of it. What are you hiding? Who are you really? The real trick in this world (it's not really a trick), is to not need a mask at all. The real you faces the real world without any masks to confuse or change reality, and makes a real difference just using their brain, their gifts and their plan to be a better person and keep creating a better world. I'm not sure who said it (could have been me), but if you want to change the world, change yourself first.

Chapter Eleven
WHY NOT YOU?

So, it's three things: A need, learning your strengths/weaknesses/wiring, and a plan. Would that make your life simpler? There is a lot of work involved in those three things, but the growth and the joy are totally worth it.

I have a final question for you. Why not you? Every single person deserves a chance to be a winner, and yet life, unfair to the end, says otherwise. Life seems to want to dictate who the winners are, and all too often, it's the very few who get to the top of something, or the ones who seem to make the most money. I think I'll decide for myself who I think the winners and losers are.

When I golf on the weekends, mostly the courses are surrounded by beautiful houses, well into the millions of dollars, and the thing I notice most is that for the most part, they are empty. Nobody is using the pool, the grounds, or the house. It's just empty. Makes me think that even on the weekend, they are out trying to pay for that house, and it's costing them their weekend to do it. Winner? Not in my book, because I don't see balance. Houses and grounds and pools are useless without people to enjoy them.

Maybe it's time to stop looking for ways to feel bad about yourself and recognize what makes you happy. Examine your life and see what your strengths are and find ways to be working on those strengths. That's what real winners do, that's the life you really want to lead.

Chapter Twelve
A Warrior's Life

The last thing I want to leave you with is living a warrior life. Now you don't have to go out and weaponize yourself, you don't need to sign up for a martial arts or self-defense course–that is not the kind of warrior I'm talking about. The warrior I'm talking about is comfortable in their own skin. They don't feel the need to put on any mask to interact with the world, and they don't expect you to feel that same need when interacting with them. They know their strengths and weaknesses, and they are doing their best to eliminate, or at least minimize, their weaknesses, but they are also happily engaged in growing a better warrior.

A warrior understands that a better life awaits when you think your way through life instead of reacting your way through life. A warrior understands that things given are easily discarded, because while you did nothing to earn them, you also attached no importance to them. A real warrior understands that when you think your way through life, you will realize that some things are worth working for, sacrificing for, even subduing your ego for, and that pursuit is your vehicle for growth.

• • • • ● • ● • • •

When you didn't want to do something, but you did it anyway, you overcame and grew. When you were mad at someone, but you realized they were acting out of habit and were able to let that anger go, you overcame and grew. The more you overcome and grow, the more you realize that in return, life will give you gifts that are important and can't be bought. Things like a high self-esteem, where you realize your worth, and are not thrown off by mean-spirited or otherwise broken people who think they need to feel better by downing others. Things like a high respect for who you are and how far you've come, so you won't be talked into doing stupid things that could ruin your life or others'

THE SWEET SPOT

lives. Things like a high self-awareness, so you make your own decisions instead of being influenced unduly by the media, or even well-meaning friends that are just trying to control a narrative.

There are so many instances of gifts that life is ready to adorn you with, but you aren't paying attention because you've grown up letting people tell you what to do your entire life. Remember the habit thing and how controlling that can be? Think about your life before you started reading this book. How long has it been since you were able to make an important decision all by yourself? When was the last time you stood alone, confident in who you are, confident that you have educated yourself on this decision enough that you know it's the right one for you, and despite what some of your friends, some of your family, and maybe even some of your co-workers may say, you happily make that decision alone? I like to think that could and should be your future.

I don't want you to think that I'm advocating for setting yourself apart from everyone else, leading a monk's existence because you don't need anyone else. Far from it. I think it's a good idea to ask for advice and different opinions on different subjects, but at the end of the day, you have weighed the pros and cons, you have done your due diligence to educate yourself and it is you who has final say on your life, then you alone make that decision. It's vitally important to learn to trust yourself and your decisions, but in order for you to do that, you must learn to make decisions for yourself–just you, no one else–because that decision will lead to knowledge, lead to growth, and lead to a better you. Interested?

• • • • • • • • • • •

The greatest attribute or quality that a warrior must possess is curiosity. Now don't confuse true curiosity with the thing that killed the cat. That wasn't really curiosity, that was nosiness, sticking your nose into other people's business, and the cat deserved it. Real curiosity is a weapon that a warrior uses to think their way through the world instead of reacting blindly to it. I'll give you an example: We were teaching a class at one of the hospitals that we service and one of the women in the class, who was relatively new to leadership and this was the first time she had experienced professional trainers, seemed to be hoping we would solve her problem for her. She asked for our help to solve a problem she was having with one of her direct reports. When we asked her what the problem was, she got a little emotional and said, "She doesn't like me."

Well, there was no way we were going to let that go, so we started probing, and it turns out that about one month into her new leadership position, and without any meaningful conversation that the leader could remember, one of her direct reports started treating her like she was angry with her–silly things like not answering questions, walking the other way when they saw each other, talking about her behind her back, etc. When we asked what, as a leader, she had been doing about those behaviors, she told us she was completely freaked out by it, and it had driven her to be almost office bound because of it. She would find herself not walking the halls and watching her nurses in action, all because she was afraid of running into her problem child.

I simply asked her if she was curious about why she was being treated this way, and when she said of course she was, I got to say, "Brilliant, you are going to solve your problem". She agreed to set a date with her problem child and she wrote down on a piece of paper two questions: 1. Are you mad at me? 2. What do I need to do so we can get beyond this?

I must say, I struggled a little because it was 30 days before we were to meet again, and while patience is a virtue, I still need to get better with patience. Anyway, we get to the meeting, and by the look on her face I could tell she had solved her problem. She was bursting to tell us, and we all were bursting to hear it. Turns out they could have both used being curious. The problem child couldn't even remember what the incident was that caused her to get so mad at her supervisor, but because she didn't know how to process that, she went almost an entire year holding onto anger and divisiveness. You already know the supervisor's reaction, so we asked what it was that was needed to move forward. Turns out a simple apology did the trick, and now the two get along really well. They are very good problem solvers when they put their collective minds to it, and they both wish they would have been curious sooner.

· · · ● · ● · ● ● · ·

As I've said before, life is messy; we don't always get all the information that we would like especially in the time frame that we need it, and without having all the information at our disposal, we simply fill in the gaps from our experiences, our prejudices, our feelings, and our current state of mind, and because we are in a reactive state, the fill-ins are usually negative. Any further conversation that could potentially solve the problem isn't even on the table–only our righteous anger is. Is that the best way to handle yourself in today's world? I get it–your habits aren't just in place to supposedly make your life easier, they are also in place to protect you, unless your habit is reactive anger, then those habits will harm you and make your life more difficult than it needs to be.

This world requires you to be a thinker to succeed. You have to be in control of yourself and use your brain to solve problems and grow. If you use anger to get your way, you may get away with it once, but people quickly tire of angry people, even if the angry people are right. Angry people may get to the point, but they certainly don't consider other people's feelings as they make their opinions known. Angry people may get things accomplished, even for long periods of time, but they leave such devastation in their wake that very quickly, people find ways to disconnect, disengage or worst of all, rebel.

Along with curiosity, I ask you to get comfortable with forgiveness. People really struggle to forgive or to ask for forgiveness, but because you are going to be a true warrior, you are going to have to forgive some people, and ask to be forgiven by some others. It is a very emotional act to forgive or ask to be forgiven. It requires you to think beyond you and consider others. It requires you to be logical and unemotional so you can see what it is that you want to accomplish, and to genuinely either forgive or be forgiven.

Another thing about forgiveness is that there are always two sides to it, and you only get to control one side. What I mean is, while you may ask to be forgiven, and you are genuinely sorry for whatever happened and your role in it, the other person can decide to not forgive you and continue to carry their grudge for however long they deem necessary.

The other part of that is that someone else may have committed a grievance against you and doesn't care about you forgiving them. So, what's your role in forgiveness now? Well, while you can't control others' thoughts or actions (and you shouldn't want to), you can control your own, and you must be authentic in your actions. Only ask for forgiveness when you are truly sorry for your actions in someone else's life, convey that you never want to be the reason for anger or sorrow in someone's life, and you will do better in the future (and then do better), and as if they could find it in their heart to forgive you. While you can't control their response, you have done the right thing. You have considered

THE SWEET SPOT

someone else as important as yourself, and you have asked for grace—not an easy thing for anyone.

Likewise, if you felt wronged, whether the other party agrees or not, you have to state your case, why you felt wronged, and let the person know that you are going to forgive them, wipe the slate clean, and start over. You must do this even if the person feels that you are out of your mind and that they didn't wrong you. It isn't the forgiveness, or the being forgiven that grows a warrior, it is the subduing of your own ego in order to consider other people's journeys and growth that grows the warrior.

Like they say, forgiveness is not for the weak—it is only for the strong! Last thing in this thread. This works for everyone! It works for adults, it works for children, it works for different genders, and it works for different cultures. It works for everyone that has a brain and would like to see if they can use it to live a better life.

So be curious about life. Ask more questions and seek to understand before you react or think. Be someone who wants growth to result from all the stuff you're having to deal with, and don't be naïve enough to think that it will all be sugar and roses from now on. Being a warrior and finding your *SWEET SPOT* isn't about protecting yourself from the world. It's about opening up and unapologetically letting the world see the real you. It's about understanding how the world works and how you can find happiness and growth from that.

Remember, the *SWEET SPOT* is a need inside of you for change, pursuing your strengths and weaknesses until you more fully understand you, and then planning your future so that growth and joy are daily parts of your life. Start learning and growing your warrior mentality, use what you've read to really learn about yourself, start a plan, and go find your *SWEET SPOT*!

www.ingramcontent.com/pod-product-compliance
Lightning Source LLC
Chambersburg PA
CBHW070303100426
42743CB00011B/2320